W9-BPK-058

299
WU

TALES OF THE DEAD

ANCIENT EGYPT

Written by Stuart Ross
Consultant Dr. Joann Fletcher
Illustrated by Inklink & Richard Bonson

LONDON, NEW YORK, MUNICH,
MELBOURNE AND DELHI

SENIOR EDITOR Simon Beecroft
ART EDITOR/STORY VISUALISER John Kelly
ART DIRECTOR Mark Richards
PUBLISHING MANAGER Cynthia O'Neill Collins
PUBLISHER Alex Kirkham
PRODUCTION Jenny Jacoby
DTP DESIGNER Eric Shapland

First published in Great Britain in 2003 by
Dorling Kindersley Limited, 80 Strand, London WC2R 0RL
A Penguin Company

03 04 05 10 9 8 7 6 5 4 3 2 1

Page Design Copyright © Dorling Kindersley Ltd

All rights reserved. No part of this publication may be reproduced,
stored in a retrieval system, or transmitted in any form or by any
means, electronic, mechanical, photocopying, recording, or otherwise,
without the prior written permission of the copyright owner.

A CIP record for this book is available from the British Library.

ISBN 1-4053-0187-2

Color reproduction by Media Development and Printing Ltd
Printed and bound in Italy by L.E.G.O.

Discover more at
www.dk.com

ACKNOWLEDGMENTS

Richard Bonson painted the town (p.6-7), Egyptian society (p.8-9), pyramids (p.10-11), pyramid interior
(p.12-13), house of the dead (p.16-17), temple of Sobek (p.18-19), and large boat (p.22).

All other artworks, including graphic novel, painted by Inklink.

The author would like to thank the pupils of King Ethelbert's School, Birchington;
Dulwich College Prep School, Coursehorn; Finham Park School, Coventry;
and North Curry Primary School, Somerset, for their valuable input in the
preparation of this book.

CONTENTS

Stone tablet carved with hieroglyphs (picture writing)

It is early morning in Egypt and the air is alive with sounds: the shouts of sailors in their boats, the clutter of shopkeepers laying out their wares, the steady creak of ploughs being driven through the fields...

The dusty streets are busy with shaven-headed people. A wealthy official in white linen glides by, his jewellery glinting in the sun. From the desert sands rise gleaming pyramids and monuments, while deep within brightly painted temples inscribed with a mysterious picture writing, sneering statues of terrifying gods stare, unblinking.

A scribe

Servants attending to noblewomen

This is Egypt 4,000 years ago, when its mighty civilization was at its height. For three millennia, the ancient Egyptians flourished along the banks of the River Nile, transforming the dry desert into a land of wonders. Finally, attacked from north and south, during the first millennium CE this glorious civilization gradually crumbled away...

The many buildings, pictures, objects and texts tell us a great deal about life in Ancient Egypt. Using this wealth of treasures, we have brought

Female musicians

the amazing Egyptians back to life in these pages. Here you will meet royalty, courtiers, scribes, priests, servants and tomb-robbers, and hear the tales of ordinary people, long dead. Just watch out for the sinister snap of the crocodile – and beware the Curse of Sobek!

TIMELINE

1969

US astronauts land on the Moon

1492

Columbus sails to America

1206

Genghis Khan conquers Asia

410

Roman Empire collapsing

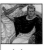

44 BCE

Death of Julius Caesar

PRESENT DAY

2000 CE   1000 CE   0 CE

THE CURSE OF THE CROCODILE GOD

The story takes place in the year 1795 BCE during the reign of the female pharaoh Sobekneferu. Methen lives in a town near Hawara in the Fayum region of Lower (northern) Egypt. Look out for the many details of Ancient Egyptian life on every page, from clothing and hairstyles to buildings and everyday objects.

STORY CONTINUES ON NEXT PAGE

I NEVER EVEN WANTED TO GO.

FATHER MADE ME.

IT IS THE WISH OF LORD INI TO MEET YOU, METHEN.

"MY NAME IS METHEN, and this is my friend Madja. Our lives are in great danger! We are entangled in a fiendish plot hatched by a corrupt official. As the son of a respected priest, nothing in my life has prepared me for this. My days have been spent at scribe school, learning to read and write hieroglyphics. Madja is a humble serving girl in a nobleman's court. Like me, she is thirteen years old but our paths had never crossed... until the evening of the banquet at Lord Ini's palace.

LAND BY THE RIVER

The civilization of Ancient Egypt flourished in North Africa from about 4000 bce to 332 ce. It grew up on a strip of fertile land, never more than a few miles wide, that lay on either side of the River Nile. Fed by rains falling to the south, the Nile snakes through the African desert for about 1,600 km (1,000 miles). This slender ribbon of life-giving water supported a remarkable people whose achievements still amaze and astonish all who behold them.

1153	c.1799	c.2050	c.2585	3100
Death of Rameses III, the last great pharaoh	Pharaoh Sobekneferu comes to the throne.	Montuhotep II reunites Egypt after years of turmoil	Building of the Great Pyramid at Giza begins	King Menes unites Egypt

1000 BCE 2000 BCE 3000 BCE

CONTINUED FROM PREVIOUS PAGE

2 ROOF LIFE

Flat roofs made a cool extra room in hot weather – an ideal place to cook meals, eat and sleep. Children played games on flat roofs, too, and would run and jump from one to another!

3 BAKED BRICKS

Houses were made of mud bricks baked in the sun. The mud was taken from the banks of the Nile. A mixture of lime and water was often used to whitewash the walls so that sunlight would be reflected, keeping the rooms inside as cool as possible.

1 MAIN GATEWAY

The only way in and out of the walled town was through guarded gates. The gates were closed at night to protect against roaming gangs attracted to the rich settlements of the Nile valley.

TOWN LIFE

Methen and Madja live in the same town, although their lives are worlds apart. Like many towns in Ancient Egypt, theirs is surrounded by high walls, like a giant fort, and its houses are crammed together in unplanned streets. The Egyptians also built large, planned towns beside their great building projects, such as pyramids or temples, where thousands of workers lived.

WHY DOES LORD INI HAVE POWER OVER YOU, FATHER?

HE IS MY LORD.

YOURS TOO, METHEN.

AND THE OVERSEER OF ALL THE PRIESTS IN THE SOBEK TEMPLE.

HE IS ALSO CLOSE TO PHARAOH SOBEKNEFERU.

I'D BETTER WATCH WHAT I SAY.

I WILL TAKE YOU TO HIM NOW.

WE CROSSED THE CROWDED ROOM.

THEN I SAW HIM...

MY LORD AND MASTER.

LORD INI.

WELCOME, MY FRIENDS.

MY SON - METHEN.

FATHER, WHO IS THAT MAN WITH LORD INI?

SHH! QUIET.

4 BARGAIN HUNTING
Shoppers bartered with stall-keepers for their wares. Almost everything was on offer, from servants to sandals. Shopkeepers generally lived in the rooms above their shops.

8 LUXURY TRAVEL
A nobleman is carried by servants in a special chair called a litter. This mode of transport was reserved for the pharoah and other important people.

7 COOLING HOLES
Windows had no glass or other covering. To keep rooms cool and free of dust and flies, small holes were left high up in the outer walls.

6 NOBLEMAN'S HOUSE
Wealthy Egyptians like Lord Ini lived in large houses or palaces. The inside walls were often brightly painted with ducks or lotus flowers (a type of water lily).

5 FURNITURE
As wood was scarce and expensive, most homes had little furniture: just three-legged stools, beds and small tables. Only rich people had chairs.

STORY CONTINUES ON NEXT PAGE

WHAT WERE YOU SAYING TO THAT **SERVANT**, METHEN?

NOTHING.

THE WELL, BY THE KITCHEN GATE.

CAN YOU MEET ME TOMORROW, AFTER SUNSET?

WHERE?

CAN I HELP YOU?

I CANNOT TALK NOW.

HE TOLD ME IT WAS KENAMUN, THE CHIEF EMBALMER.

HE WAS SO **UGLY**.

I WATCHED HIM SLIDE INTO THE **SHADOWS**.

HE MET SOMEONE...

...A **SERVING GIRL**.

SHE LOOKED **TERRIFIED**.

SHE SAW ME WATCHING...

...AND HEADED **TOWARDS ME**.

C...CAN I HELP YOU, SIR?

PRISONERS

Prisoners brought to Egypt during its conquests in Nubia (to the south) and the Near East were put to work, often in royal workshops. These workers could obtain their own freedom or the freedom of their children. Sometimes, the descendants of these prisoners attained high-ranking positions in the Egyptian government or in the military.

PRISONERS FROM NUBIA

SERVANT

FAN BEARER

EGYPTIAN SOCIETY

Everyone knew their place in Ancient Egyptian society. At the top was the king, or pharaoh, who was considered a son of the gods. On the next rung were his family, his wives and children. Below them came the top government officials, generals and priests – they were equally important because religion and politics overlapped. After the petty officials and officers came the ordinary people, farmers and labourers. Servants like Madja worked for wealthy people.

WORKER'S FAMILY

SONG AND DANCE

No feast was complete without a troupe of musicians, acrobats and dancers. Some performers were well respected and earned their own money working at official functions.

DRESSER

MUSICIAN

SINGER

ACROBAT

WORKERS

Ordinary men and women worked in the fields and on the pharaoh's building projects – such as when he or she ordered a pyramid-tomb or rock-cut tomb to be built. As money didn't exist in Ancient Egypt, workers were paid in food and goods.

CONTINUED FROM PREVIOUS PAGE

THE NEXT EVENING, I **CREPT** OUT...

SHE WAS **WAITING** FOR ME.

PSST! IN HERE!

THANK YOU FOR COMING. MY NAME IS **MADJA**.

I AM **METHEN**.

YES, I ASKED OF YOU AT LORD INI'S PALACE.

YOU DID? WELL, ER, WHAT IS YOUR TROUBLE?

IT IS NOT EASY TO SPEAK ABOUT. I – AM – BEING – FORCED INTO **MARRIAGE**.

TO WHOM WILL YOU BE GIVEN?

LAST NIGHT YOU SAW HIM ...

BY SOBEK'S HOLY CLAWS! NOT THAT SNAKE, **KENAMUN**??!!

IT **CAN'T** BE SO!

THE VERY MAN. I AM TO SHARE THE HOUSE OF THE **CHIEF EMBALMER**.

THE MAN WHOSE HANDS PULL OUT THE **ENTRAILS** OF THE **DEAD** BY DAY...

EGYPTIAN MARRIAGE

BRIDE AND GROOM

Madja's enforced choice of husband would not have been unusual in ancient Egypt. Most marriages were arranged by the girl's father and, to a lesser degree, mother. Girls would marry at around 13 years of age and boys at 16. A scribe could draw up a contract giving equal rights to both husband and wife. Producing children was the main purpose of marriage, and couples used all kinds of potions, prayers and spells to get the gods to bless them with offspring. Childless couples often divorced.

HIEROGLYPH FOR "SCRIBE"

SCRIBE

THE ARMY

Egypt's army fought off invaders and captured slaves. Soldiers were ordinary labourers ordered into the army by the king. They carried swords, javelins and daggers, but wore little armour.

GENERAL

SOLDIER

PRIESTS

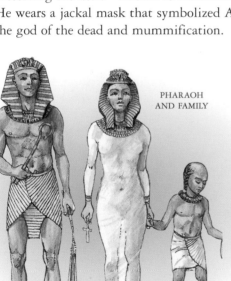

Methen is one of the few people in Ancient Egypt to learn the complicated picture writing known as hieroglyphs. He will become an official writer (called a scribe), and, eventually, a priest, like his father. Kenamun's role as Chief Embalmer is to preside over the ceremonies for preserving the dead – known as mummification. He wears a jackal mask that symbolized Anubis, the god of the dead and mummification.

PRIEST

CHIEF EMBALMER

MINISTER

PHARAOH HATSHEPSUT

THE ROYAL FAMILY

PHARAOH AND FAMILY

The Egyptians believed that their kings, or pharaohs, were semi-gods, and therefore above the normal rules of society. Most pharaohs were men, but a handful of women ruled Egypt at several times. One of the most powerful and longest reigning female pharaohs was Hatshepsut, who ruled for about 15 years, until her death in 1458 BCE. To help her to fit in, she dressed in the traditional clothing of male rulers, and even wore a false beard!

STORY CONTINUES ON NEXT PAGE ➤

HE HAS YEARS ENOUGH TO BE MY GRANDFATHER. AND HE OWNS A WIFE AND THREE MISTRESSES ALREADY...

SHHH!

WHO IS IT?

ONE MOMENT...

...IT'S HIM!

KENAMUN!

TOMBS FOR THE GODS

The pyramids are the most impressive of all ancient Egyptian monuments. These burial tombs for the king-gods, the pharaohs, and their queens originally stood at the heart of a complex of funeral monuments and buildings. Raised between 2686 and 1550 BCE, it was some time before the 'true' pyramid shape emerged.

2 REED COFFIN
As wood was rare, the first coffins were woven out of reeds.

Burial pit beneath mound

Pottery vase

1 BURIAL
The Egyptians originally buried their dead in simple graves dug in the sand.

3 MOUND GRAVE
By 4,000 BCE, important graves were marked by mounds. Bodies were buried with objects they might need in the next life.

A chapel and a statue of the tomb owner lay inside.

Burial chambers were built deep underground.

THEY BEGAN TO **CLIMB UP THE PYRAMID!**

WE **FOLLOWED** THEM, KEEPING OUR DISTANCE.

4 MASTABA TOMB
Mastabas (from the Arabic for 'bench') were rectangular tombs for royal burials c.3100–2686 BCE. They then began to be used for non-royal burials. The burial chamber was built underground, often carved from rock. The visible part – the actual bench-shaped mastaba – was built on top from brick or stone.

5 STEP PYRAMID, SAQQARA
The first pyramid was built by the gifted architect Imhotep for Pharaoh Djoser (2667–2648 BCE) at Saqqara. The six-step pyramid was 60 metres (200 feet) high, and represented a staircase to the sun-god. It was made of 330,400 cubic metres (11.7 million cubic feet) of stone and clay – enough to fill 120 Olympic-sized swimming pools!

CONTINUED FROM PREVIOUS PAGE

KENAMUN AND TWO OTHER MEN PASSED BY US.

THEY CREPT OFF INTO THE MOONLIGHT.

WHAT ARE THEY UP TO?

THEY WERE HEADING TOWARDS THE **PYRAMID.**

I NOTICED THAT ONE OF THE MEN HAD A **LIMP.**

ALL THREE CARRIED WOODEN LEVERS.

10

6 BENT PYRAMID, DASHUR

Pharaoh Sneferu (2613–2589 BCE) built three pyramids in an attempt to construct a true pyramid with sloping sides. He began one of the two at Dashur, with tombs inside, but the structure started to collapse before it was finished. To stop it giving way completely, the top was finished at a different angle from the base – producing the Bent Pyramid. His third pyramid at Dashur became the first true pyramid.

7 THE GREAT PYRAMID, GIZA

The reign of Pharaoh Khufu (2589-2566 BCE) saw the construction of the impressive Great Pyramid at Giza—the largest pyramid ever built.

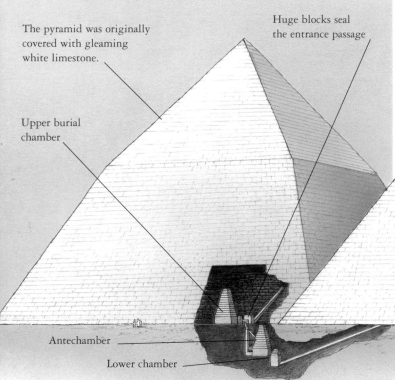

The pyramid was originally covered with gleaming white limestone.

Huge blocks seal the entrance passage

Upper burial chamber

Antechamber

Lower chamber

Grand entrance gallery

King's burial chamber

Abandoned chamber

Gold cap stones

Passageway

Underground chamber

Secret entrance

STORY CONTINUES ON NEXT PAGE

8 MORTUARY TEMPLE

Pyramids were part of a funerary complex in which a member of the royal family was laid to rest and worshipped as a god. Worship took place in a mortuary temple built near the pyramid. Its focus was a statue of the king-god, tended by priests day and night.

Inner rooms

Open courtyard

Pillars made of granite

A kilometre (0.6 mile)-long stone causeway reached towards the Nile

9 ROCK TOMBS

Pyramids might be impressive, but they were an obvious target for tomb robbers. During the New Kingdom (1550-1069 BCE), kings and other royalty were buried in tombs cut out of solid rock. Rock tombs, like the one built for King Tutankhamun and his treasure in the Valley of the Kings, were thought to be more secure.

Entrance

Tutankhamun's gold shrine was so large it nearly filled one whole room of his tomb

SECRET DOOR

The entrance to a pyramid shaft was normally on the north side. It was carefully disguised with the same brick or stone as the rest of the construction. However, as many people had helped build the pyramid and then witnessed the royal funeral, the doorway was not exactly a secret.

INTO THE PYRAMID

Ancient Egyptian pharaohs oversaw the construction of a pyramid during their lifetime so it was ready when they died. Each pyramid was different, reflecting individual taste and wealth. The body was accompanied by valuable treasures, so the temptation to rob a royal tomb was almost irresistible. Yet, as Methen knows, the penalty was death.

Priests used this secret passage to exit the pyramid after the main door and burial chamber had been sealed.

Methen and Madja hide in one of the shafts designed to line up with important stars in the night sky.

LISTEN... SOMEONE APPROACHES!

QUICKLY! UP HERE...

DON'T MOVE!

THE PASSAGEWAY WAS **DARK** AND **HOT**.

THE AIR WAS **STALE**.

False burial chamber to confuse robbers

IT WAS **KENAMUN**!

False paving over deep shaft

TRAPDOOR

Tomb robbers had to watch their footsteps. To catch the unwary, pyramid builders laid false paving over deep shafts. When the robber trod on the thin cover, it gave way and he fell headlong into a dark prison – which soon became his grave.

CONTINUED FROM PREVIOUS PAGE

HEADBANGING

One way to keep out tomb robbers was to wedge heavy stone blocks above the entrance shaft. When these blocks were disturbed (for example, by opening a door), they fell down and buried the intruder.

HE WAS CARRYING A SACK.

LET US **SEE** WHERE THEY HAVE BEEN.

WE SAW A LIGHT AHEAD.

IT'S THE BURIAL CHAMBER!

TUNNELING DOWN

Often, the entrance to a burial chamber was sealed with massive slabs of stone. Unable to move them, cunning robbers found a way in by removing the ceiling bricks and jumping down from above.

STORY CONTINUES ON NEXT PAGE →

Chariot stored in pieces in secondary treasure chamber

BURIAL CHAMBER

The mummified body of the dead king was laid in the burial chamber at the heart of the pyramid. The chamber was built from granite blocks for greater strength and was shaped like a little house. Everything the deceased might need in the afterlife was packed in it, including jewellery, food and, even, instructions on how to make sure they made it to eternal happiness.

Massive granite construction for security and to resist the weight of the pyramid above.

Funerary texts (special hieroglyphics) cover the walls of the burial chamber.

Main entrance to the tomb is lower than head height

Stars on the ceiling symbolize the heavens

Pitched roof for added strength

Pottery vase – some vases in burial chambers contained wine and expensive perfumes

Furniture for the pharaoh to use in the afterlife

Heavy stone coffin that protected the body

Wooden coffin painted with eyes of the god Horus – this was so that the deceased, placed on his side within the coffin, could watch the sun rise.

WE'RE TRAPPED. BURIED ALIVE!

IT WON'T MOVE!

THE ENTRANCE STONE HAS BEEN PUT BACK INTO PLACE!

THEN IT GOT WORSE.

TERRIFIED, WE RETRACED OUR STEPS.

WE MUST LEAVE.

THESE JARS HAVE BEEN OPENED.

IT WAS CLEAR WHY KENAMUN HAD COME.

IT WAS THEN THAT I SAW THE WRITING ON THE WALL.

WHAT DOES IT SAY?

"CURSED BE HE WHO DESECRATES MY TOMB."

"MAY THE GREAT GOD SOBEK TEAR HIS LIMBS..."

"...AND CAST HIS SOUL INTO THE PIT OF EVERLASTING PAIN."

ARE YOU ALRIGHT?

MAKING MUMMIES

CONTINUED FROM PREVIOUS PAGE

WE PUSHED AS HARD AS WE COULD.

BUT THE STONE WOULD NOT **MOVE**.

WE MUST FIND SOMETHING TO PUSH IT OPEN WITH.

AT THE DOOR TO THE **BURIAL CHAMBER**, WE STOPPED.

THE CURSE...?

WE HAVE **NO** CHOICE.

The Egyptians preserved their dead by a process called mummification. It was thought to allow people to live forever after death. The Egyptians believed that everyone had a *Ka* and a *Ba*. The *Ka* was the person's double, or soul, and the *Ba* was like the spirit. In order to live forever, the *Ka* and *Ba* needed to be reunited in the body after death. So it was important to stop the body rotting. A decayed body meant an unhappy *Ka* – and misery in the afterlife.

THE *BA* BIRD

NOSE TRICK
To remove the brain, a hook was pushed through a nostril and rotated vigorously for 20 minutes. This broke up the brain, turning it into a glue-like substance that could be drained out through the nose. The skull was then turned over and washed out with preservatives.

Iron hook

Broken-up brain ran out through the nose

Preserving resin

The heart was left in the body

IMSETY PROTECTED THE LIVER

HAPY GUARDED THE LUNGS

QEBEHSENUEF GUARDED THE STOMACH

DUAMUTEF WATCHED OVER THE INTESTINES

PRESERVING THE ORGANS
When people were mummified, the lungs, stomach, intestines and liver were removed. These organs were washed, dried, bandaged and placed in special containers called canopic jars. The jars were sealed with lids in the form of each organ's guardian deity and placed beside the mummy inside the tomb.

1

MUMMY CASES
The finished mummy was decorated with jewellery and make-up, and bandaged. Then it was placed in a wooden coffin, often human-shaped. Coffin cases of royalty and other important people were highly decorated with significant designs and hieroglyphs.

WE WILL HAVE TO USE THE **COFFIN**.

I KNEW THAT MADJA WAS **TERRIFIED**.

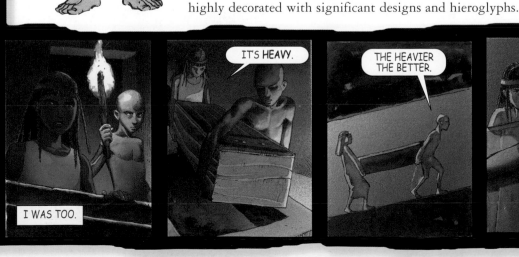

I WAS TOO.

IT'S **HEAVY**.

THE HEAVIER THE BETTER.

AIM AT THE DOOR.

ONE, TWO, THREE...

DRYING OUT

The key to good mummy-making was getting the body as dry as possible. This was done by placing it on a special embalming table and smothering it with natron, a salt-like substance found in the desert. The body remained covered for 40 days, during which time it lost about 75 percent of its weight.

Chief embalmer wears a Jackal mask symbolizing Anubis, the god of the dead.

Models of Osiris, the god of death and rebirth, were placed in tombs.

Embalmer pours natron onto body

Chief embalmer leads magic chants

MUMMY CASE

1 To restore its natural shape, the dried-out corpse was stuffed with fresh natron and rags scented with sweet-smelling oils.

2 Artificial eyes were inserted into the skull. The body was coated with resin and tightly bandaged to protect it.

3 Bandaging the body was a religious ritual that took 15 days. The linen bandages, often made from old clothes, were soaked in resin to stiffen them.

4 Protective amulets or charms were placed on the body in key places such as the heart and wrapped up with the bandages.

5 Securely tied with hundreds of metres of bandage, and protected with magic charms, the body was now a suitable residence for the eternal *Ka*.

STORY CONTINUES ON NEXT PAGE

WHO KNOWS WHAT KENAMUN WOULD DO.

WE **HAD** TO FIND OUT WHERE KENAMUN HAD HIDDEN THE **STOLEN TREASURE**.

HE WILL SUSPECT HIS **OWN MEN**.

WE HAD EXPOSED KENAMUN'S SECRET ENTRANCE.

LET US GET **AWAY** FROM THIS PLACE.

THUD!

CRASH!

HELP!

LORD **SOBEK** PROTECT US!

STORY CONTINUED FROM PREVIOUS PAGE ▶

HOUSE OF THE DEAD

Kenamun is the chief embalmer in the House of the Dead — a building or tented enclosure where bodies were mummified. They were sometimes built in the desert outside towns because of the smell and the flies. The mummification process was a religious ritual that lasted 70 days.

6 CLEAN ON THE INSIDE
After the organs had been removed, the body cavity was cleaned out and rinsed with palm wine. Meanwhile, the organs were stored in canopic jars.

5 ORGAN DONOR
Watched by the Chief Embalmer, a jackal-headed priest of Anubis, the god of the dead, the body was washed. It was then cut open and the brains and internal organs were pulled out.

7 DRYING OUT
Empty corpses were laid on wide, wooden or stone embalming tables and covered with natron. This technique was developed from earlier methods of drying in hot sand.

1 GRIEVING RELATIVES
When a dead body was carried to the House of the Dead, the entire family came out to wail and cry — sometimes with hired mourners to add professional tears.

2 BODY IN A BOX
The body arrived in a plain wooden box.

3 WELCOMING PRIEST
A priest welcomed the family at the door and showed them into the entrance foyer.

4 ENTRANCE FOYER
Shielded from the sight (but not the smell) of the grisly operations going on inside, the family registered the body and selected a style of mummification and coffin.

STORY CONTINUES ON NEXT PAGE

8 BIRDS OF PREY
Eagles swooped overhead, eager to snatch a tasty morsel of human flesh.

9 TAKING A BREAK
While a corpse is carried from the drying room, the workers take a break in their covered rest area. Here they ate, drank, played board games – or just took a nap.

10 BIRD SCARER
The priest employed young boys to scare away birds of prey and other desert scavengers, such as wild dogs and cats.

11 SPICING IT UP
In this corner, the heart was packed with bags of spices and herbs, and padded out with linen and sawdust!

12 BANDAGES
When the first bandages went on, every finger and toe was wrapped individually. Sometimes, body parts were mixed up, so the body of one person might be mummified with someone else's head!

13 COVER UP
Each mummy was wrapped with as many as 20 alternating layers of bandages – in total, up to 250 square metres (2,690 square feet), or half the size of a football pitch! At the same time the linen is brushed with resin.

17

NEXT MORNING, I ACCOMPANIED **FATHER** TO WORK.

I HAD TO **SPEAK** TO HIM.

FATHER IS A PRIEST...

...IN THE **TEMPLE OF SOBEK**.

THE VERY **GOD** WHOSE **CURSE** LAY **HEAVY ON MY HEAD**!

I KNEW IT WOULD NOT BE EASY TO TALK TO HIM.

YOU KNOW HOW **BUSY** THE TEMPLE IS...

1 STONE NEEDLE

Stone obelisks outside the temple pointed to the sun and were carved with inscriptions in praise of the gods and the pharaoh.

2 ON GUARD

Crocodile-headed statues guarded the entrance to the temple. They wore headdresses of sun disks and feathers on their horny heads.

3 GATEWAY

A ceremonial gateway of tapering towers joined by a bridge, known as a pylon, rose above temple entrances. Only priests, the king and high-ranking officials could go beyond this point.

4 PHARAOH POWER

The temple walls were covered with scenes of the pharaoh's great victories – real or imaginary.

AND FATHER IS ONE OF THE MOST **IMPORTANT** PRIESTS.

HIS DUTIES ARE MANY.

WHILE HE PREPARED THE **OFFERINGS**, I WAITED FOR MY MOMENT.

I FELT THE PRESENCE OF **SOBEK** ALL AROUND ME.

IT MADE ME **SHIVER**.

11 SACRED SPACE
Only priests and the pharaoh could approach the shrine of Sobek, lying at the dark, mysterious heart of the temple. Only the priests were thought to have the power to understand the god's wishes.

10 FEEDING THE GOD
Just like people, gods in Ancient Egypt needed to eat. The priests prepared regular meals, which were laid before the image of the god in the morning and evening and cleared away later. The priests were permitted to eat the leftovers, once the god had had its fill!

9 PRIESTLY SANCTUARY
Only the important priests and the pharaoh were allowed to enter the temple's inner rooms. They performed religious rituals in these rooms.

TEMPLE CITY
The largest temples were rebuilt and enlarged over many centuries, until they covered several acres. They were important centres of commerce, as well as religion. The largest temples employed dozens of people, owned farming land and mines, and even engaged in foreign trade. The walled temple itself – a maze of rooms, pylons, courtyards, shrines and statues – was surrounded by store-houses, workshops, workers' homes and priest schools.

8 VITAL SUPPORT
Giant stone columns held up the roof. They were decorated with painted designs of papyrus plants with closed flowers.

7 SACRED POOL
Behind the temple, in a safely walled-off pool, real-life sacred crocodiles lazed in the sunshine. The priests sometimes used water from the sacred lake to perform rituals in the temple.

6 TEMPLE COURTYARD
Carved crocodile images adorned the walls of the temple courtyard, which was open to the sky. Sobek was shown as either all-crocodile or half-man, half-crocodile.

5 ROYAL HIGH-PRIEST
The pharaoh was the high priest of all temples. Scenes on the courtyard walls showed him making offerings to Sobek, reminding people that their king was a vital link between them and the gods.

TEMPLE OF SOBEK

All over Egypt, people praised Sobek, the crocodile god – but the Fayum region, where Methen lives, was the god's main place of worship. Priests in the town of Crocodilopolis, for example, were so croc-obsessed, they adorned live specimens with gold, and fed them honey cakes and meat! This most ferocious of gods was also honoured in spectacular temples, where priests guarded, cared for, and worshipped the god's image day and night.

STORY CONTINUES ON NEXT PAGE

HAVE **MERCY** ON US, **SOBEK**.

THE RITUALS SEEMED TO TAKE FOREVER.

THE GOD MUST BE WASHED AND DRESSED.

ANNOINTED WITH PERFUMES

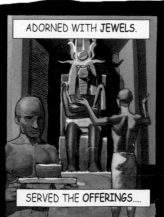

ADORNED WITH **JEWELS**.

SERVED THE **OFFERINGS**....

I COULDN'T WAIT ANY LONGER. I ASKED FATHER...

...ABOUT THE FATE OF THE **PYRAMID** THIEVES.

HIS ONLY ANSWER...

SOBEK WILL BE AVENGED.

BUT MADJA AND I HAD COMMITTED SACRILEGE, TOO.

THE RIVER OF LIFE

The civilization of Ancient Egypt depended on the mighty River Nile. Every year, between June and September, monsoon rains fell thousands of kilometres to the south and caused the river to rise and flood the surrounding countryside. The flood, called the 'Inundation', brought fresh life to the dry fields along its banks. In order to measure the height of the river and thus predict when the flood would arrive, the Egyptians used measuring devices called 'Nilometers'. The readings from Nilometers were carefully recorded.

NILOMETER

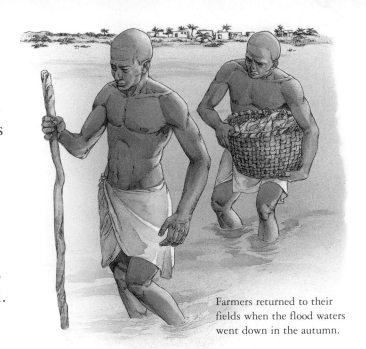

Farmers returned to their fields when the flood waters went down in the autumn.

NILOMETERS

Ruled horizontal lines were cut into steps along the Nile's banks to measure the all-important level of the river. Many temples had their own Nilometers, which were thought to gauge the god's favour as well as the Nile's height.

DISASTER FLOOD!

NORMAL FLOOD

NORMAL LEVEL

FLOOD WATERS

As the Nile's water level rose during the rainy season in Central Africa, land on either side was submerged: the higher the flood, the more land would be under water – making it fertile for planting crops. When the floods reached a mid-level, the Egyptians believed that Hapy, the god of the Nile, had smiled on them.

1 Houses were built well above the highest flood level. When the river was low, however, it was a long walk to fetch water for cooking and washing.

4 Exceptional flood levels occured only every ten years or so. The highest floodwaters could be highly damaging, washing away people's houses built on higher ground.

2 The river was at its lowest level every spring. Travelling upstream against the slow current was easy. Farmers completed the harvest before the river rose again.

3 The size of the flooded area depended on how steeply the land beside the river rose. In a normal flood year, the floods deposited rich soil washed down from the highlands. This was dug and planted in the late autumn.

CONTINUED FROM PREVIOUS PAGE

I MET MADJA THAT EVENING.

WE DECIDED TO SEARCH KENAMUN'S BOAT.

THERE IT IS.

LISTEN... SOMEONE'S DOWN THERE.

...THEY'VE FOUND TWO OF KENAMUN'S MEN...

TWO GUARDS WERE TALKING.

NAKHT AND IAHAMES, WITH THE LIMP...

"THEY WERE FOUND IN THE DESERT..."

"NO MARKS ON THEIR BODIES."

LORD INI SUSPECTS POISON.

I WONDER WHO THEY GOT ON THE WRONG SIDE OF?

Tall papyrus reeds grew best in the Nile delta.

Papyrus stems are an unusual triangular shape.

The tough outer edges were cut away.

The inner part of the reed was soaked in water and cut into strips. Each strip was beaten with a wooden hammer to soften and flatten it.

STORY CONTINUES ON NEXT PAGE

Harvested reeds were tied in bundles and carried to the workshop.

Softened strips were now laid across each other and beaten again so they meshed together.

PAPYRUS

The papyrus reeds that grew beside the Nile were made into boats, baskets, ropes and a type of paper. Papyrus paper (just called 'papyrus') was first made over 5,000 years ago and was used for almost 3,500 years. The sheets were not bound into books, but were joined together in long rolls. Normally, just the inside was written on and the outside was left blank.

A sheet of papyrus

Finally, sheets of papyrus were pressed with weights as they dried out.

Only scribes knew how to write the complicated hieroglyphics.

ROPE STRETCHERS

After farmland had been under water for months, farmers often had little idea where their fields had been. To solve this problem, surveyors, scribes, supervisors and inspectors would arrive with ropes to measure the land at low water. They kept a record of the measurements, and then, after the floods had gone down, the 'rope stretchers' returned and measured out the fields again. These officials also fixed the amount of tax the farmers had to pay.

ONE SOUND...
ONE MOVE...
AND YOU DIE!

...I DIDN'T REALISE HOW QUICK!

NOTHING HERE!

KENAMUN KNOWS MUCH ABOUT POISONS!

LOOK, THE GUARDS ARE LEAVING.

KENAMUN SHOULD BE HERE BY NOW.

LET'S GO AND LOOK FOR HIM.

RISKING ALL, WE MADE OUR WAY TO THE BOAT.

HURRY!

I KNEW WE HAD TO BE QUICK...

NOW, WHY WOULD MY **BETROTHED** BE SEARCHING MY PRIVATE BOAT?

PERHAPS SHE HAS BEEN LED **ASTRAY** BY HER **NEW FRIEND**....

I WILL TEACH YOU NOT TO **SNOOP** INTO MY AFFAIRS.

HOW WOULD YOU LIKE TO **SWIM** HOME?

HA! HA! HA!

MY BLOOD WAS AS **ICE**.

Sail made of papyrus

Bundles of papyrus reeds tied together with ropes

Steering oars

Mast made of wood from acacia tree

Bundles of papyrus reeds tied together with ropes

FUNERAL BOAT

PRIVATE BOAT

Trees were scarce in Egypt's desert kingdom, so a sailing boat with a wooden mast was a status symbol. Only wealthy officials like Kenamun and Lord Ini could afford one. Larger private boats had cabins to shelter their owners from the heat of the sun.

ON THE NILE

The River Nile was Egypt's "super highway". People went everywhere by water, in many different types of boat. The smallest craft were simple fishing canoes made of papyrus reeds. The largest vessels were merchant ships carrying goods to and from Egypt and container barges carrying statues and large stones for building. River travel was so vital that the symbol (hieroglyph) for 'going north' was a ship with sails down, while 'going south' was a ship with sails up.

SO THIS WAS LORD SOBEK'S **REVENGE** FOR THOSE WHO **DISOBEYED** HIM!

FORGIVE ME, METHEN. PLEASE! I BROUGHT THIS UPON YOU.

DON'T SPEAK LIKE THAT, MADJA...

SILENCE!

WE **DRAW CLOSE** TO THE PLACE.

PREPARE THE VAGABONDS FOR THEIR **SWIM**!

MERCHANT SHIP

LONG-DISTANCE
SAILING BOAT

PLEASURE BARGE

WAR SHIP

CARGO
BARGE

HUNTING IN THE NILE

Although most food was provided by farming, Egyptians also fished and hunted in the Nile. Fishermen took to the waters in simple boats made of reeds to catch fish with hooks or nets. Teams of men in boats hunted hippos with spears (*left*) – these wild animals could be a danger to people in boats and to their crops on land. Egyptians also hunted wild birds, such as heron and duck, with special throwsticks (*below*).

Pole used to
push boat along

Throwstick hurled
at wildfowl

STORY CONTINUES ON NEXT PAGE

23

THE GREAT HOUSE

The word 'pharaoh' originally meant 'great house', the place where the king lived. Later, it came to mean the ruling king him or herself. The pharaoh was chief priest and judge, army commander and ruler all rolled into one. Meeting the pharaoh at court must have been a genuinely nerve-wracking experience!

BIG-GAME HUNTING

Kings liked to be thought of as great hunters. To help their heroics, animals were rounded up and held in game parks. Here the royal hunters could be sure of making a spectacular – and simple – kill. Their victims included wild bulls, lions and even ostriches.

RED CROWN   WHITE CROWN   DOUBLE CROWN   BLUE CROWN

VULTURE AND COBRA HEADBAND

CROWNS OF EGYPT

In Ancient Egypt, crowns were probably made of coloured cloth, leather or metal. Pharaohs had many styles of crown to choose from. The earliest was the White Crown of Upper Egypt. When a single king ruled the whole land, this was combined with the Red Crown of Lower Egypt to make the Double Crown. Alternatively, they could wear a blue crown adorned with golden discs or a stripy headband called a circlet.

CONTINUED FROM PREVIOUS PAGE

FIND THEM, **IDIOTS!**

LOOK OUT!

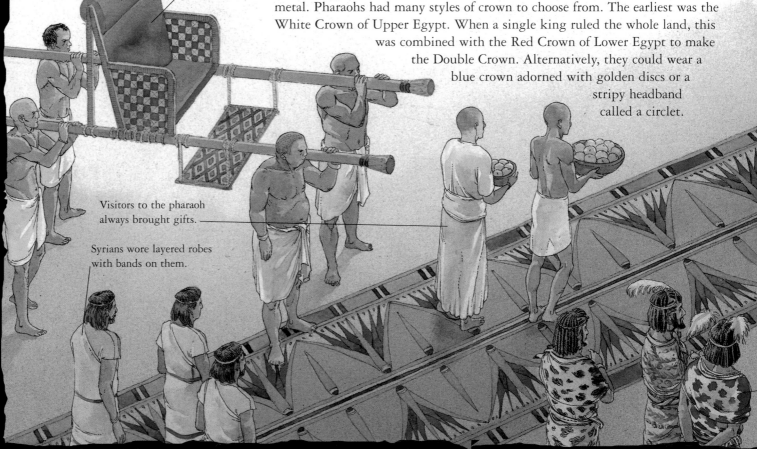

The queen was often carried on a special chair called a litter

Visitors to the pharaoh always brought gifts.

Syrians wore layered robes with bands on them.

HURRY!

WE'RE NOT SAFE YET – **LOOK!**

QUICK – IN HERE!

WE HID IN THE PAPYRUS REEDS **ALL NIGHT.**

WE WOKE AT **DAWN** AND CHECKED THAT WE WERE **SAFE.**

WHAT SHALL WE DO **NOW?**

The pharaoh was always accompanied by his private guards, as well as by courtiers and musicians.

In public, the pharaoh held a crook and flail – the symbols of royal power.

MORNING RITUAL

The pharaoh was expected to win the favour of his fellow gods so that Egypt would prosper. He performed a ritual every morning, burning incense to the sun god Amon-Ra.

Scribes kept written records of important events.

The floor in the throne room was tiled and painted with murals depicting beautiful gardens.

People from the lands bordering Egypt came to pay their respects to the Pharaoh to ensure peace between their countries.

Courtiers waved fans made of dyed ostrich feathers to keep the pharaoh cool.

People from Libya typically dressed in clothes made of brightly coloured animal hides with feathers in their hair.

THRONE ROOM

The most splendid place in the pharaoh's palace was the throne room. Here, the pharaoh held royal audiences, when officials and nobles came to him to read reports about the country or make requests. On these occasions, the pharaoh sat on a covered platform, like an altar or a stage. Since the pharaoh was a son of the gods, the throne room was a holy place.

STORY CONTINUES ON NEXT PAGE

THE MIGHTY SOBEKNEFERU!

IT WAS THE PHARAOH!

WE ALL DROPPED TO THE FLOOR.

I COULDN'T **BELIEVE** IT!

JUST THEN, TRUMPETS **BLARED** AND THE DOORS WERE **FLUNG OPEN**.

WE MUST TELL LORD INI...

HE WILL SAVE US.

WE RETURNED TO THE TOWN...

AND HEADED FOR THE **PALACE OF LORD INI**.

I EXPLAINED WHO MY FATHER WAS...

AND WE WERE **GRANTED** AN **AUDIENCE**...

WITH HIS LORDSHIP.

CONTINUED FROM PREVIOUS PAGE

Feather of Truth

KEEPING THE PEACE

In general, the Egyptians seem to have been a law-abiding, practical people who based their law on common sense. Many laws were only clearly written down in the Late Period (747-332 BCE). Throughout the early Ancient Egyptian period, high officials often acted as judges, although in later times specialist judges were appointed who wore a gold pendant. The king, of course, was the supreme judge in any dispute.

GODDESS OF JUSTICE
The goddess *Maat* represented justice. She was worshipped throughout Egypt – even by other gods!

Curved sword called a *khepesh*

The Medjay thickened their hair with wax to form a kind of protective helmet!

Theft

Inheritance disputes

Street fights

SETTLING QUARRELS
Town councils of senior citizens normally settled day-to-day squabbles. The council, known as the *kenbet*, heard both sides of the case before making a decision. Scribes kept a record of the proceedings. It was also possible to ask a god or goddess, via a priest acting as an oracle, to decide a case. The priest would then let the accused know the god's answer!

The word 'Medjay' became the ancient Egyptian term for 'policeman'.

POLICE FORCE
The Egyptians had two types of police – guards and enforcers. Groups of guards patrolled the desert to fend off raiders. The task of guarding frontiers, mines and other important sites was largely in the hands of the Medjay – a fierce tribal people from Nubia, the land south of Egypt. The job of enforcing the law, arresting wrongdoers and punishing the guilty was carried out by men known as *sa-per*.

THE PHARAOH **GLOWERED** AT US.

WHY ARE THESE **CHILDREN** HERE, LORD INI?

LORD INI EXPLAINED OUR BUSINESS.

I DO **NOT** LIKE WHAT I HEAR.

GO, BRING **KENAMUN** HITHER!

AFRAID TO MOVE, WE WAITED.

WHEN KENAMUN ARRIVED, HE DENIED **EVERYTHING**.

IT IS A SHAMEFUL **FALSEHOOD**, YOUR MAJESTY!

WHERE IS THE **EVIDENCE**?

I SWEAR BY **SOBEK** THAT WE ARE **HONEST**.

An official reads the charges - the tax inspectors are accused of stealing taxes for themselves (taxes were paid in goods, such as corn).

Scribes record the proceedings.

Guards force the prisoners to kneel.

Prisoner with hair grown back

The guilty men are tied to a pole and flogged in public.

The servants carrying out the punishment sarcastically describe the beating as a "nice present"!

PAINTED FRIEZE SHOWING THE TRIAL AND PUNISHMENT OF CORRUPT TAX INSPECTORS

PUNISHMENT

Punishments were intended to be short, sharp shocks. The commonest form of punishment was a public beating, with the criminal kneeling and tied to a short pole. The number of strokes depended on the crime. Punishments for more serious crimes included mutilation (cutting off the nose, for example), wounding or death. Less violent punishments included fines, confiscation of property and exile (being sent to live outside Egypt). As the Egyptians considered all foreigners to be completely uncivilized, exile was a particularly shameful punishment.

Armed guard

Overseeing official, wearing a wig to mark his high status.

Guards wielded papyrus reeds.

Ropes bound the prisoner's arms and wrists.

Prisoners were tied to a pole.

Prisoners' hair has grown in gaol.

Scribes kept records of the charges against prisoners and the number of lashes they received as punishment.

STORY CONTINUES ON NEXT PAGE

WHY WAS IAHAMES KILLED, SIRE?

DID HE KNOW TOO MUCH?

IGNORANT SLAVE! SLAY HER!

HARSH WORDS, KENAMUN.

YOUR BETROTHED IS SHE NOT?

I BEG YOUR MAJESTY...

ORDER A SEARCH OF THE HOUSE OF THE DEAD.

SO BE IT.

WE WILL SEARCH THE HOUSE OF THE DEAD.

BUT, CHILDREN, IF NOTHING BE FOUND - YOU DIE!

CRAFTWORKING

A rt and craft was a serious matter in Ancient Egypt. At the back of an Egyptian's mind was a nagging worry that the universe and all its gods and people might one day pass away. They believed that if artists and craftworkers created perfect examples of things, this was less likely to happen. Unsurprisingly, top painters, sculptors and craftworkers could become rich and respected citizens.

BOW DRILL FOR BORING HOLES

PLUMB LINE FOR CHECKING VERTICAL LINES

CHISEL

SET SQUARE

WOODEN MALLET

ADZE FOR SMOOTHING SURFACES

The molten silver is poured into a clay mould.

Blowpipes used to increase the fire's heat

Paints were made from minerals such as copper and iron.

Workers used a sharp tool called a bradawl to make a starter hole for drilling.

Wooden chair with ornamental back

Wooden model of a servant to go in a tomb

Finishing off a vase

SILVER WORKERS

Craftworkers used copper and bronze to make tools, weapons and jewellery. Silver was rare and more precious than gold – the gods' bones were said to be made of silver! Metalworking was a hard job, involving the carrying of many heavy loads. Metal foundries were dirty, smelly and often dangerously hot, due to the open fires beneath the furnaces. Safety precautions were almost nonexistent.

WONDER WEAVE

Egyptian linen cloth was famous throughout the ancient world. The thread was made from the flax plant then woven into cloth on broad looms. Extra-special cloth had gold thread woven with the linen.

Linenworkers lift finished cloth from a loom.

SKILLED ARTISTS

Since the making of images was so important to Ancient Egyptian society, artists and specialist craftworkers were important people. They enjoyed a much higher standard of living than farmers or ordinary craftworkers such as potters. However, much of the basic work was done by lowly helpers, leaving those in charge to add the finishing touches – and get all the praise.

CONTINUED FROM PREVIOUS PAGE

WE WERE ESCORTED TO THE HOUSE OF THE DEAD.

KENAMUN WAS MUTTERING AND CURSING.

SCANDALOUS...!

A MERE SLAVE!

THE SOLDIERS BEGAN TO SEARCH THE PLACE.

THEY OPENED POTS...

SEARCHED THE NATRON STORES...

AND UNRAVELLED BANDAGES.

THEY WERE THOROUGH, LOOKING ALMOST EVERYWHERE.

WE HAVE FOUND NOTHING, SIR.

Comic panels (top row):

STOP HIM!

UP CLOSE, THE BODY WAS REVOLTING...

LET ME BE RIGHT, LORD SOBEK!

THEN, JUST AS A ROUGH HAND GRABBED MY SHOULDER....

LOOK!

STORY CONTINUES ON NEXT PAGE

HEY!

IT HAD TO BE WORTH A TRY.

I HAD TO THINK OF SOMETHING!

THERE WAS ONE OTHER PLACE...

LORD INI ORDERED US TO BE LED AWAY TO THE PLACE OF EXECUTION!

AS I SAID!

Cone shows that this person was wearing perfume

Make-up box

MAKE-UP

In Ancient Egypt, both men and women wore make-up. Thick green or black eye make-up was the height of fashion, as was red lip paint and rouge for cheeks. Many paintings show women with cones on their heads (*above*). Some experts think these cones were scented wax that melted and ran down their wigs. In fact, the cones were probably symbolic, showing simply that a person smelled delightful!

Wooden comb

Polished silver mirror

WORTH COPYING

When 19th–century Westerners first returned with Egyptian artefacts and furniture, the ancient style became the height of fashion from London to Moscow. The workmanship, however, rarely matched that of the originals.

GOLDEN CHAIR

Chairs were symbols of authority and only important people could afford beautiful seats like this one. Made for Tutankhamun's aunt, Sitamun, its wooden frame is overlaid with gold and silver.

BOARD GAMES

The Egyptians enjoyed board games, including Dogs and Jackals, played with pointed sticks carved with dog or jackal heads. The game of Senet was also immensely popular: everyone played it, from kings to servants.

Senet board

29

CONTINUED FROM PREVIOUS PAGE

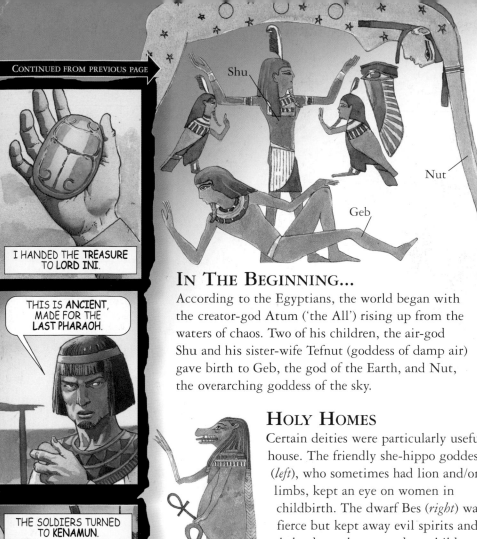

Shu

Nut

Geb

EYE SPY

Horus, the pharaohs' own god, once had his missing left eye kindly restored by the goddess of love. After that, the Horus-eye (or *wedjat*-eye) became a very popular symbol of healing and protection. Horus-eye jewellery was often buried with the dead.

3 HEART OF THE MATTER

In the Hall of Judgement, the heart of the deceased was placed on one side of a balance. To the ancient Egyptians, the heart was the centre of a person's personality, containing all their memories. This is the reason the Egyptians took special care to leave the heart in the body of the deceased.

2 THOTH

Holding a reed pen, the ibis-headed god, Thoth, recorded the verdict on the deceased person's soul. Thoth was the god of writing and knowledge. He was associated with the moon, too, because his curved ibis beak looked like a crescent moon.

IN THE BEGINNING...

According to the Egyptians, the world began with the creator-god Atum ('the All') rising up from the waters of chaos. Two of his children, the air-god Shu and his sister-wife Tefnut (goddess of damp air) gave birth to Geb, the god of the Earth, and Nut, the overarching goddess of the sky.

HOLY HOMES

Certain deities were particularly useful about the house. The friendly she-hippo goddess, Tawaret (*left*), who sometimes had lion and/or crocodile limbs, kept an eye on women in childbirth. The dwarf Bes (*right*) was fierce but kept away evil spirits and helped couples to produce children. People often wore a carving of him around their necks for luck.

FACING THE GODS

The Egyptians worshipped hundreds of gods and goddesses, who were responsible for everything that happened, from the flooding of the Nile to the appearance of the sun in the sky. The Egyptians also believed that the gods judged them after death in the Underworld, a grim region where monsters lurked in dark corners. Only those who had lived good lives escaped.

1 YOU ARE CHARGED...

Deep in the Underworld, a dead person (or, rather, his spirit, or soul) met the King of Death face to face. Quivering with fear, he listened to a list of the bad things he had done in his lifetime. He must then deny the charges. If successful, he moved on to the even more-frightening 'weighing of the heart' ceremony....

Devourer of the Dead

I HANDED THE TREASURE TO LORD INI.

THIS IS ANCIENT, MADE FOR THE LAST PHARAOH.

THE SOLDIERS TURNED TO KENAMUN.

I CAN EXPLAIN...

SUDDENLY, HE PUSHED LORD INI AWAY....

HE KNOCKED OVER A TABLE OF NATRON POTS...

AND HUMAN BODIES!

A CLOUD OF NATRON STUNG OUR EYES...

SEIZE HIM!

WHILE KENAMUN SPRINTED OUT OF THE HOUSE OF THE DEAD.

HE RAN AT GREAT SPEED TOWARDS THE RIVER....

WHERE HE STOLE A SMALL BOAT!

HEY!

4 PERFECT BALANCE

Anubis weighed the heart of the deceased – the essence of their being – against the feather of *Maat*, which represented goodness and truth. If the two balanced exactly, the dead person was said to have spoken truly. He could then approach the throne of Osiris. The failures wished they had never existed....

5 THE INCORRUPTIBLE JUDGE

Osiris, the god of death and rebirth, presides over the judgement of a spirit, with his sister-wife Isis standing beside him. In legend, Osiris was once a living pharaoh who was murdered by his evil brother, Seth. However, the devotion of Isis allowed Osiris to defeat death and become a god.

Isis

THE END

6 DEAD WATCHER

The god Anubis – jackal-headed and the colour of a rotting corpse – played a part in everything that happened after death. He kept an eye on mummification and offered a helping hand when a dead person was judged in the Underworld.

Osiris

Anubis operates the scales of truth

Horus

The feather of truth (the scales' other pan holds the human heart in a vase)

The Devourer has the head of a crocodile, the front body of a lion, and the rear end of a hippo

7 DEVOURER OF THE DEAD

The Egyptians' greatest fear was to be dead for ever. This was the hell that awaited the hearts of those who failed the tests of the Underworld. They were thrown to the merciless Devourer of the Dead – a gruesome hybrid of crocodile, hippo and lion – that lurked hungrily beside Anubis' scales.

8 MEETING OSIRIS

The hawk-headed god Horus stood beside Osiris. Horus was the god of the sky, who was embodied on Earth by the living pharaoh. (This is why the pharaoh was part-god.) Horus took the successful spirit to the throne of Osiris – where eternal life began.

THE CURSE OF LORD SOBEK HAD COME TRUE.

IT'S NOT SAFE....

HA! THEY'LL NEVER CATCH ME NOW!

THE OWNER OF THE BOAT EXPLAINED THAT HE HAD BEEN MENDING A LEAK!

WHAT?!

I'LL HAVE TO SWIM!

BY THE BLOODY BEAK OF MUT...?

NOOOO!

INDEX

DELETED SCENES These additional panels were not used in the final story due to lack of space.

PAGE 14
Methen and Madja try their hardest to move the entrance stone.

PAGE 24
Escaping from Kenamun – and some dangerous hippos in the Nile.

PAGE 25
Lord Ini seated on his throne when the children ask for his help.

PAGE 28
Madja and Methen under armed guard in the House of the Dead.

PAGE 30
Kenamun realises the game is up and breaks away from the soldiers.

PAGE 30
Spears narrowly miss Kenamun as he runs for his life over the desert.